For Mom

My beautiful, amazing mother is the reason for this little book. For years she has encouraged me to share my love of home and family with others. So now I am. I am not a published writer, doctor, therapist, or psychologist. I am a former elementary school teacher turned stay-at-home mom to four incredible blessings here on Earth, and one in Heaven.

The thoughts in this book are taken from posts I wrote for my blog, *Afternoon Coffee and Evening Tea*. I compiled some of the eleven hundred plus posts I've written since starting my little space in 2012 to make this book as a gift for my mother.

My mother is beginning her journey down the unforgiving path of Alzheimer's Disease. She is a constant presence in my life and continues to guide and support my family and me every single day. This little book is for her, and I pray she will hold it within her beautiful hands, the same ones that held each one of my children and me.

I hope that the thoughts in this book encourage readers

to embrace the gifts of motherhood, home, and family. But I understand not everyone will share my thoughts and ideas within these pages. Each mother's experience is unique to her and her family, and so I hope that by reading my words, each woman will find something she can take away and adapt to her own life, while living her blessed vocation of motherhood.

Afternoon Coffee

Thoughts on Motherhood, Family,
Home, and All Things Cozy

Billie Jo Stoltz

Contents

A Note From Billie Jo

Thank you so much for reading this little book. The following passages are based on entries from the blog I began in 2012, *Afternoon Coffee and Evening Tea,* where I write about my favorite things: motherhood, family, home, and all things cozy. It may be helpful if I introduce you to my family before you start. Our family consists of my husband Steve and myself, our daughter Madison, 22, and her husband Nicolas, our daughter Peyton, 19, our son Rhett, 17, and our daughter Flynn, 9. We also have two furry family members, our dogs Kirby and Mocha. The selections are organized in order by the date they were written, so as to tell a chronological story. Pour a cup of your favorite coffee, tea, or cocoa, settle in and get cozy. Enjoy!

Afternoon Coffee

Every afternoon I sit down and enjoy a cup of hazelnut coffee. I have ever since Madison was a baby. I began setting aside that special little time for myself when she was old enough to take a regularly scheduled nap each day. Even though it was almost 16 years ago, I remember covering her up in her crib, patting her back, and tiptoeing out of her room. I remember thinking of all the things I could accomplish while she was asleep. I could run the laundry, tidy up the TV room, write out bills. Then I thought about leaving all those things for a few moments and relaxing with a cup of coffee. Wouldn't all those tasks still be there waiting for me?

Sixteen years and three more sweet babies later, I still say yes. I deserve a few moments in the day to take care of myself. How can I care for my family if I'm not caring for myself first? Some days my mind races with things I need to do. However, the thought of my steaming cup of coffee always wins. I pour a cup, hold the warm mug in my hands, and savor the first sip. I sit and look at magazines, read a chapter of my book, or even gaze out the window. Simple, I know, but my afternoon coffee makes me happy.

Being An "Older" Mom

August 27, 2012

My oldest daughter Madison and my youngest daughter Flynn are almost thirteen years apart. As an older mother, I am not as active with Flynn as I was with Madison. After all, I had Madison when I was twenty-seven and Flynn at forty. It takes me a little longer to get off the floor after playing Little People with her. I sit outside and watch her and the others play ball rather than play myself. And I may encourage a bit more television snuggle time together with her as opposed to another afternoon walk. That's the reality of being blessed with a toddler at the age of forty-two.

All these things, however, are offset by the positive aspects of being an older mom. I am so much more relaxed with Flynn than I was with poor Madison. After all these years, I know that every fever isn't strep throat, and every fall doesn't result in a broken bone. I know that Flynn will eventually go in the potty, and I don't need any fancy incentive kit with bright stickers to help things along. We have a potty. She plays with it. Someday she will use it. I know that if she doesn't eat carefully-measured, organic food from matching dishes complete with coordinating silverware, she'll survive. Sometimes she even has ice cream for breakfast and a Pop-Tart for dinner.

The parenting book I dug out when I was pregnant with Flynn sits untouched on my nightstand. When I started this incredible journey called motherhood, I needed others to tell me how to be a good parent. Now, I KNOW how to be a good mom. I've learned from my children what they need. I didn't find it in parenting books. Although they are useful at times, like when your toddler has a weird looking rash, and you forget about two-year molars. What my children need is me. They need a confident, relaxed, happy mommy. It doesn't matter if that mommy is twenty-seven and pushing a stroller three times a day, or forty-two and snuggling on the sofa watching Cinderella one more time.

Oh. And my sincerest apologies to you, my dear Madison, for not allowing you to eat Pop-Tarts or watch The Rugrats. Sorry for all the unnecessary trips to the doctor. And sorry for the no chocolate until you were four-years-old-rule. What was I thinking?!

Our Crib

September 10, 2012

I was changing bedsheets the other day, and as I was smoothing the sheets in Flynn's crib, it hit me. Hard. I wouldn't be changing sheets on this beautiful crib much longer. I realized that my baby is almost three. And while I have never had a hard and fast rule about when I take a baby out of a crib, I kept my two older girls in it until about three years old. My Rhett stayed in his crib until he was almost three and a half. I remember thinking that he couldn't start school while he was in a crib even if it was only three-year-old preschool!

I don't know what made me think about Flynn moving to a big bed. Maybe it's her third birthday looming ahead. Perhaps it's the fact that Peyton is getting ready for a room redo, and Flynn will be sleeping in her room. Maybe it's because my Madison is almost sixteen, and I remember so vividly the day Steve and I shopped for a crib.

In any case, I realized that this piece of furniture, this beautiful crib which has been a part of my life for almost sixteen years, will most likely no longer be needed. That bothers me. I can't explain exactly why, except to say that our crib signifies the baby years. It holds so many beautiful memories. I am not one to rush a baby out of a crib into a toddler bed. I love a baby in a crib. I love seeing a baby all snuggled safe and sound and protected. I love waking up and seeing a little face peeking out at me through the rails. I love hearing a baby calling me when nap time is over, and the smile on that baby's face when I come into the room. I love the sight of a baby's outstretched arms waiting to be picked up and snuggled.

I will miss this time of my life, which seems to have passed so quickly. I remember when Rhett moved into his big boy bed. I kept the crib up in his room as long as I could in hopes that it would be needed again. Even though we eventually took it down, I wouldn't let Steve put it in the downstairs storage area. I kept it upstairs in the small attic space near our bedroom. I couldn't part with it. And by the grace of God, I did get to use that beautiful crib again for my baby Flynn. I can't believe it's been almost three years since that glorious day when we set it up again, this time in our own bedroom.

Now, as the clock ticks down on my baby years, I enjoy every moment of dusting and changing sheets in that crib. I stand beside it while Flynn is sleeping. I run my hand over the teeth marks that my Madison made while she was teething all those years ago. I see Peyton giggling as I pretended not to be able to find her when she played hide and seek with me. I remember so many nights of reaching under the bed skirt of the crib to find Rhett's binky in the dark because he somehow managed to fit it through the slats. And I am sad at the thought of it all coming to an end. But I'm also grateful that I've had this beautiful crib in my home for all these years. And who knows, maybe someday it will be used again. Although, at almost forty-three and with four c -sections behind me, that seems unlikely. But as my sweet husband recently pointed out to me, our grandchildren will have a wonderful crib filled with many sweet memories waiting for them.

My Girls Make Me Happy

September 24, 2012

Madison, Peyton and I were sitting in Peyton's room last night just before bed. We were talking about school and friends and all that typical girl stuff when Madison said, "Peyton is my best friend, Mom." And then Peyton added, "Madison is mine." That moment was one of those extraordinary mom moments. You know the ones. They are the moments you thank God for, the ones you want to wrap tightly and store in that very special place in your heart. The moments that years from now, you'll pull out and remember and smile with tears in your eyes. I went to bed with a smile on my face last night.

My two sweet girls are each other's best friend. What more could a mother ask for? My girls make me happy.

Dandelions

May 5, 2013

Sometimes it takes something small, a quick unexpected moment in an otherwise ordinary day to help us stop and not only look at something, but actually see it. Sometimes it takes someone else, someone young enough to have a mind full of wonder and a heart full of excitement to remind us to stop and not only see something but also enjoy the beauty of it.

As I was taking our puppy Kirby out first thing this morning, I barely noticed the numerous dandelions beginning to pop up in our yard. I went back in and continued my routine, feeding the puppy, unloading the dishwasher, getting breakfast. Suddenly, Flynn ran and grabbed my hand. She was bursting with excitement and begging me to come to the door with her. When we reached the door, she gazed out the window and whispered, "Look at all the beautiful flowers, Mom!" She was in awe of the bright yellow bursts of color interspersed among the blades of green grass. And she was right. When I looked and saw them, I realized they were beautiful.

We stopped what we were doing and went outside. Flynn ran and giggled. She enjoyed and appreciated the beauty of those simple dandelions and in doing so, made me stop and see them too. I saw them not as annoying weeds in need of mowing, but as beautiful signs of spring. And then I ran and grabbed my camera. I wanted to see those beautiful dandelions not merely through the lens of my camera, but the eyes of my child. And that is precisely what I did.

In The Blink Of An Eye

May 12, 2013

Madison and her best friend Jeffrey had a great time at Prom Saturday night. I was so happy for them and was in awe of how they've grown from those two little preschoolers playing spaceship on our swing set into two young adults who are old enough to drive to dinner, Mass, and Prom.

Oh, how my heart smiles when I think of a day not that many years ago when these two shared a little sweet dinner date. I remember standing outside, taking a picture of the two of them. I remember saying to Jeffrey's mom, my friend and neighbor Sharon, "Someday they'll be going to prom together!" And we laughed thinking about that far off day. I got those pictures developed, and we smiled at how cute these two were on their very first date. And then I tucked the photos away and continued on with my life as a young mother.

I answered the door when Jeffrey knocked to see if Madison could come out and play. I cleaned my house. I grocery shopped. I went to church with my little family. I gave birth to more sweet babies. One day, I moved with my family to a new home outside of town, and no longer answered the door to little Jeffrey's knocks. I cooked the meals. I decorated for Christmas and Easter and Halloween. I baked cookies and did laundry. I picked my kids up from school. I read books. I gave birth to one more sweet soul. I took trips to Disney World and the beach. I gave baths and brushed hair. I clipped coupons and took walks. I slept. And I blinked.

Then one day I heard a knock at the door. I opened it to see a face I remembered but did not recognize. It was Jeffrey, wanting to know if Madison could come and go for a ride. Somehow, someway, as I lived my life in what seemed to be the blink of an eye, this young boy who danced in my living room to Britney Spears and swam in my pool for hours on end and ate peanut butter sandwiches at my kitchen table had grown into a young man. And he asked my Madison to his Senior Prom. He told us he wouldn't have dreamed of taking anyone else.

And so now, as I look back at pictures of my Madison and her friend Jeffrey, I realize just how quickly life passes by, and I cherish every minute, knowing even the smallest of moments will become a beautiful memory in just the blink of an eye.

Keeping Track

June 9, 2013

I learned many things about life and raising children from my wonderful mother. One such example is the simple task of using notecards to keep track of important milestones in my children's lives. My mother used them for all five of her girls. I have a yellowed, worn notecard with my mom's distinguishable handwriting detailing moments in my life tucked away with my special things.

Beginning the day we come home from the hospital, I jot down notes on a notecard once every week for the first year. It's so easy to take a few minutes once a week and write down the baby's accomplishments, feeding schedule, and milestones. It isn't fancy or complicated, but it sure comes in handy as a reference and a memory keeper!

Despite having no scientific proof, I believe that from the moment each of my precious newborn souls snuggled in my arms, time moved quicker than before. I lived in the insulated, beautiful, sometimes chaotic moments of sweet smelling babies, late night rocking chair snuggles and first days of preschool, blissfully unaware or unwilling to admit that those days wouldn't last forever. I was confident that I would never forget the details surrounding my child's first smile or giggle or first bite of food, but trust me, I did. Taking those few minutes once a week means I will have those precious moments documented forever.

After the first year, I jot down random events as they occur, being sure to date each one and record the child's age. I have one for Madison's first playdate, Peyton's first time baking brownies, Rhett's first time telling me he loved me, and Flynn's first time in the swing. I also keep a note card on each birthday with a few notes about the past year, always amazed that another year has passed so quickly.

I also keep a separate box for each child for sickness. I can't tell you how glad I am to have those little notes about fevers and symptoms when I make those late night phone calls to the doctor.

Individuality

July 29, 2013

Mothering is a vocation full of constant learning. I am by no means an expert, nor do I claim to be, but through the years, I have learned something significant about the balance between consistency and individuality.

It first occurred to me when I saw that, once again, my sweet Peyton had straightened the entire downstairs. Peyton is my little nanny/personal assistant/housekeeper. She folds laundry, sets the table, takes care of Flynn, and helps with the overall running of the house. I began to think that Madison never does these things without being asked. Again and again. And again. Then I had a moment of clarity, an honest to goodness light bulb moment.

As much as it's essential to be fair and consistent in regards to chores and responsibilities, it's also equally important to recognize each child's individuality and interests. Children are individuals. Each child has his or her interests, strengths, and passions. It's hard to remember that sometimes, and children often get grouped together and are expected to respond and behave in the same way.

As I looked around that morning and saw the work Peyton had done, I realized that Peyton enjoyed straightening and baking and pushing Flynn on the swing for hours on end. Rather than become irritated that Madison rarely seemed to help with these things, I thought about all the things she DOES do. Madison loves to help me with my hair and makeup. She always makes sure I look my best when I have a special place to go. Madison paints my nails and Flynn's too. She is also a very social person and spends a lot of time visiting with my mother and helping her around her house. She plans and hosts parties at the Senior Center too. These are wonderful things, and I realized they are as equally important as the household chores Peyton does for me.

Rhett also does his share, and while it isn't the same as the girls, it is part of who he is and what he enjoys. Rhett is very close to my father and spends a great deal of time talking to him on the phone about movies and baseball and soccer. He is extremely loving and patient when my sweet father repeats the same question or gets slightly confused. Rhett also makes sure to keep the refrigerator well stocked with my favorite drink of choice, Cherry Coke.

Flynn, as young as she is, shows tendencies toward organizing and home keeping. She loves to help with the laundry and is a pro at making my coffee. Oh, and did I mention she loves to Swiffer the kitchen floor?

This doesn't mean my children always love what they do. Of course, Madison still has specific responsibilities like unloading the dishwasher or vacuuming. Rhett still needs to be reminded to replace the garbage bag several times. And

Peyton still needs to be prodded to call her grandma on the phone, because that's just not her thing. It means that I've realized how important it is to meet my children where they are and to celebrate their gifts, strengths, and interests. It also means that I've learned that my children seem to do a job better - and with less grief - when it is something they enjoy. Motherhood is indeed a blessing, a vocation, and a chance to learn as well as teach. And I thank God every day for allowing me to do just that.

Homeschooling

October 18, 2013

As we continue our journey through our newest adventure, homeschooling, I am finding the importance of embracing each child's individuality to be even more evident. I am spending more one-on-one time with each of my children in a different setting; the classroom, and in doing so, I realize how essential it is to remember that I have four unique children.

I preface this by saying that I don't feel one is right and the other wrong. It is merely an observation and a tool to enable me to nurture and educate each child in a way that is best for him or her. For example, Madison is laid back. She is easy going and relaxed about everything in life, including schoolwork. Madison is also a very independent worker. She can play music, text, and write a paper on The Raven at the same time. And she does it all quite well. My job is to reign her in and encourage her to stay focused and interested in her schoolwork.

Peyton, on the other hand, is driven. She is driven to complete, driven to succeed, driven to accomplish. She rarely needs my help. When she doesn't understand something, however, she has no patience for anything but a quick explanation. I have found that with her, my best bet is to listen patiently, guide her to the information, and wait for her to figure it out.

Rhett is the one who requires most of my assistance. That's to be expected, as he's only in the sixth grade. Rhett is a complete mix. He desires to complete his work well, yet is easily distracted. He is also sensitive, and therefore, I need to gently remind him to focus and get things done.

My Flynn is typical of most preschoolers. She is excited, eager, willing, and adorable. She calls me Teacher and is so precious it makes my heart happy. I enjoy every moment of our time at the little white table.

I am so thankful for these amazing gifts from God. I am also aware of the fact that in giving me four children, God did not give me four identical gifts in matching wrapping paper. God blessed me with four entirely different gifts, all beautifully wrapped in uniquely different paper with various, intricate designs. My job is to unwrap and examine each one carefully, and with thanksgiving, learn how to treat each precious gift with the greatest of care.

Perspective

March 4, 2014

My Madison cannot do a cartwheel. And that's all right. I remember picking her up from school one day years ago, and she was in tears. She told me that in gym class that day, she was the only girl who couldn't do a cartwheel. As I squeezed the steering wheel tighter until my knuckles went white, I flipped through the Rolodex in my mind, frantically searching for a place where my sweet little seven-year-old could learn to do a cartwheel so all would be right in her world. And suddenly, I stopped. Something in my mind quieted that frantic voice and told me to stop. And get some perspective. I am so thankful for that moment in my life.

I asked myself if in the bigger picture of life, did it matter if Madison could do a cartwheel? If she has a burning desire to be a gymnast or competitive cheerleader, yes. Absolutely. If not, if her interests lie elsewhere, then no. I can do a cartwheel. And guess what? It doesn't matter. I haven't done one in thirty years. It does not play a role in my life. So why stress about it? Why spend hours and hours driving her to a gym and watching her practice and practice so that she can do something that other people think she should be able to do?

Peyton cannot do one either. Peyton has no interest in any extracurricular activities. At least the ones other people her age are spending hours doing. She doesn't do basketball or cheerleading or volleyball. Does this mean she is wrong? Or lazy? No way. It merely means that she has chosen to spend her time doing things she enjoys. Peyton spends her time at home. She is learning to cook, bake, plan meals, do laundry, and care for Flynn. Peyton spends her extra time babysitting for friends of ours. She loves it and does an excellent job. She also loves to read and spends hours visiting other places between the pages of books.

Rhett doesn't play basketball. Around here, young people start basketball in third grade. Rhett dutifully signed up for third-grade basketball a few years ago. He spent every Saturday that winter in an old gymnasium learning drills and skills with every other boy in his grade. He came home with pages of exercises he was supposed to practice in our basement every night. Never mind that we had a finished basement with carpet. We went to the final practice and watched as every single boy in his grade showed off skills and talents. Rhett decided that while it was ok, he had no interest in spending the rest of his school career playing basketball. And Steve and I were glad. If that were his genuine interest, if he had an innate talent and innate desire, then yes. We would encourage him to continue. But as it was, he did not.

Rhett's interest lies somewhere else. Movies. Rhett loves movies. He has a collection of over a hundred and fifty

DVDs and watches them over and over. He studies the characters and the plot lines. He follows the storylines and character developments. And he loves it. This is much more than a hobby for him. Because we allowed Rhett to pursue his interests, he found a place where he can learn more about the movies he loves. He spent so much time at the theater watching movies, the lovely family that owns it asked him to help out there. Rhett now knows how to run the films and works the concession stand. He helps sweep up after the shows and talks about movies for hours with the owners. And he loves it. Side note here: my dear father's very first job was also running movies in the local theater years and years ago.

What will the future hold for my little Flynn? If I had to guess based on her current interests, I would say something along the lines of wearing a blue ball gown and a tiara while dancing with a handsome prince.

Where am I going with all this? I'm merely stating that it's all right to say no. To all the young mothers out there who are beginning to feel the pressure to sign your preschooler up for soccer, basketball, or gymnastics simply because everyone else is, you have a choice. If your child shows an interest in or a talent for something, then, by all means, foster that. Encourage it. And sign him up. But if not, if your little one has no interest in soccer or basketball or gymnastics, then allow her to find her own interests and activities. Don't feel pressured to spend precious hours of your little one's childhood sitting in a gym or at a soccer field just because you think that's what you're supposed to do.

You have a choice. Put it in perspective. And enjoy your children's childhood, because it goes by so very quickly. Your memories remain. Make them happy ones. Be it sports or art or movies or childcare, let your child find his or her own thing. Put it in perspective. And enjoy.

My dear sweet husband said it best last evening as we pulled away from Dairy Queen with our treats made by Madison. He said he was happy for her. Some kids have sports. And Madison has Dairy Queen. And all is right with the world.

What's In A Name

March 15, 2014

My father's name was William Joseph. My name is Billie Jo. I was the fourth bundle of pink for my parents, and my mom says boy or girl, I was going to be named after my dad. I was baptized with the beautiful name Mary, after our Blessed Mother.

My husband is the seventh child in his family. Rumor has it, his mother let the other kids vote on his name. Stephen it was. His middle name is that of his grandfather. The second time I met him, I guessed on the second try that his middle name is Wilfred, after his grandfather. He told me it began with a W, so my first guess was William. Then, I made a rather blunt comment that I hoped it wasn't something weird like Wilfred. Funnily enough, it is.

I always wanted to be a mom and could not wait to name my babies. Before Madison was born, we settled on the name Shelby. Well, Steve had. But after twenty-four hours of hard labor, and an emergency C-section, I earned the automatic right of naming our beautiful new daughter. Madison it was. Her full name is Madison Marie, her middle name chosen to honor our Blessed Mother.

We never found out what our babies were going to be, but I remember having Peyton's name chosen very early on. Steve chose her name after a lovely character in a show we watched while I was pregnant. Her full name is Peyton Rose. Rose is a favorite name of mine. Peyton was a tiny little thing, and I took to calling her my little Peyton Rose.

When Rhett came along, I was shocked that he was a boy. I don't know why, I just thought that after two little ladies, I would have one more. Once the shock wore off, I chose the only name I ever had for a boy, Rhett. I named him after my favorite character from my favorite novel and movie; Gone With The Wind. Because I was so sure Rhett was going to be a girl, I had no middle name picked out for him. When the nurse asked me what his middle name was going to be, I remember blurting out that I guess it would have to be Stephen because I couldn't think of anything else! And that is how my son got his name, Rhett Stephen.

Finally, my Flynn. Our blessing from God. None of our pregnancies came easily. When we were praying for one more, we were told that we would have a slim chance of ever conceiving because my hormone levels were approaching perimenopause. Well, tell that to God, because He sent us our Flynn in His own due time. I love the name Flynn, and that was going to be it, girl or boy. Her middle name is a favorite of mine and my mother's grandmother's name. Her full name is Flynn Grace. Or, as we refer to her, Baby Flynn.

Growing Away

May 19, 2014

Yesterday it hit me. My Flynn is growing up. And not just growing up, growing away. This is always one of the most difficult parts of childhood for me. And it is purely selfish, I admit. I struggle through it with each and every child. It sneaks up on me, even though I know the day is coming. The day, the moment, when she wants and needs to break away from me. From the safety and comfort and contentment of being with me. Just me. Mommy.

You see, from the moment she was born, I loved her. I loved holding her and staring at her and knowing she was mine. I cuddled her and played with her and took comfort in the fact that she and I were a team. Mother and baby. She needed nothing more than my love and attention. We played blocks on the floor and read countless books and snuggled under the fluffy brown blanket with her milk and my coffee and watched Little Bear every afternoon.

When the big kids went outside on warm spring days, she stayed with me and watched from the window, giggling and waving at her brother and sisters. When Daddy took the big kids to the movies, she stayed home with me. I gave her bubble baths and dressed her in warm jammies and rocked her to sleep in the quiet of the evening.

When the long days of summer arrived, and Daddy took the older kids to the pool late at night, she and I stayed behind and sat on the porch swing and looked at the stars. When we went to the park and Daddy and the big kids went on the scary roller coasters, she sat in her pink stroller while I pushed her around looking at all the people.

She was happy. But days pass quickly. And children get older. Suddenly, that baby that I carried so lovingly into the house wrapped in a baby blanket is now a preschooler with long brown curly hair and a smile that lights up our lives. She loves to dance and sing and is very fond of the color pink. But that is not all that is different. My baby is a child now. I no longer have three kids and a baby. I have four children.

Yes, the moment has arrived, ever so quietly. It snuck up on me, even though this is the fourth time it's happened and I should have been expecting it. My little girl wants and needs to break away. She no longer stays inside with me on warm spring days. She puts on her shoes and runs outside with the other kids. She rides her big wheel around the driveway as fast as they do. When she comes in, she tells me all about it. And she is happy.

When Daddy takes the kids to the movies now, my Flynn goes along. She gets water and popcorn and sits in her seat and swings her legs because, of course, they're too short to reach the ground. When she comes home, she tells me all about it. And she is happy.

This summer, when the nights are warm and long, she and I will go to the pool with Daddy and the big kids. She will sit on my lap while I put on her floaties, and then she'll jump right in. When we go to the park, she will walk along beside me, holding my hand, and then run off with Daddy and the big kids to hop on all the rides. And she will be happy.

I will be happy too. I will be happy for her. Because even though I will miss that baby and the precious, happy moments we shared, I cannot keep her from what she is supposed to do. She is supposed to grow and change and learn and play. She is supposed to become the child and young person and woman that God made her to be. I am here to guide her and love her and teach her. And ultimately, let her go.

This is but the first of many times I need to let her go. Today, when she goes, it is just outside. Someday, she will go away to college. Or to a job. And one day, to a home of her own. All of my sweet children will. That is perhaps the hardest part of parenting for me. Letting my babies go. Realizing that one day, the child that my husband and I dreamed of and waited for and loved and nurtured will leave and begin anew. Just as we did, and just as a child should.

I hope and pray that when that day comes, I am ready. Ready to let each of my babies go. For now, I will take comfort in the time we spend together, and in the memories that I tuck deep inside my heart. For someday, they will be all I have. And a whole lot of grandchildren too, I hope.

It Works For Us

July 14, 2014

When my children were young, we didn't go to the pool on summer afternoons. When asked why, I would quietly explain that my little ones napped in the afternoons, and I liked to keep them on a schedule. Years ago, when I was younger, I cared what other people thought. Now, not so much. We do what works for our family. Even though I no longer have little ones that nap, we still don't go to the pool in the afternoons. It just isn't our thing. Some people do. And that works for them. Our family has a different schedule, and it works for us.

Our summer schedule has changed very little over the years. Perhaps that means it's working. During the beautiful summer days, we spend mornings outside, before it gets too hot. We like to sit on the porch while I have my coffee. The kids ride bikes, or we go for a walk. If it's very hot, we'll get out the sprinkler and water table too.

Around noontime, we come inside and get cleaned up. Peyton and I start to prepare lunch, which during the summer is our main meal of the day. This works well since

Madison works mostly from three to ten or eleven, and I like her to have a good meal before she goes to work. It's also nice to have the cooking done, and the kitchen cleaned earlier in the day so that we can relax and enjoy.

After lunch, we have quiet time. This is when the little ones used to nap, but now sometimes it is just me! We usually watch a movie or read. We are currently viewing the Disney movies in chronological order. This is the hottest part of the day, and we like to spend it indoors. Plus, I find that the kids need some time in these long summer days to just rest and renew.

In the evenings, we have a small meal and head back outdoors. Steve gets home around this time, and we take a walk or play outside with the kids. We also like to sit on the porch and visit. If it's hot, we go to the pool and swim. It's usually is empty at that time of day. Will this schedule work for everyone? Certainly not. It does work for us, and that is what matters.

Stop The Glorification Of Busy

August 25, 2014

I am not the author of this quote. I do agree with it, however, one hundred percent:

"Stop the glorification of busy." These days people wear the word "Busy" as if it were a badge of honor. More often than not, when I ask people how they are, I hear instead how BUSY they are, how much they run from activity to activity, how crazy their lives are, how they are never home. I hear how they have to run their child to soccer practice followed by dance class and flag football before a weekend basketball tournament two hours away. And yet, I hear it spoken with a sense of pride as if being busy is a symbol of status in our world today.

When Rhett was younger, I tried to plan a birthday party for him. It was next to impossible to get any of his friends to attend on a Sunday afternoon, as they had flag football and soccer practice. They were seven years old! One mother told me she didn't even show her son the invitation, because he had a flag football game that day, and he would want to miss it to come to the party! That broke my heart.

I know I sound judgmental. And perhaps I am. But it is more than that. I have very strong feelings about the importance of family, the importance of allowing children to slow down and be kids. I feel strongly about living in the moment and allowing our children to experience their childhood in a state of peace. I urge young mothers to know they have a choice. It is possible to say no to the chaos, the craziness, the anxiety-filled commotion that society portrays as the norm. It doesn't have to be the norm. In our house, it isn't. And we are happy. Very happy.

Society wants us to believe that to be happy, to be successful, to be accepted, families must be busy. They must be busy running here and there, busy sending four-year-olds to soccer camp and basketball tournaments, busy attending every single party and wedding. Children must be busy practicing high school sports twelve months out of the year, for a season that lasts six weeks, busy signing children up for three activities every season and eating dinner in the car in between events. Parents must keep busy joining every committee and group we can.

I am here to say that is not true. You don't have to fall into the trap of sacrificing your family life for society. For anything. Because childhood passes so quickly, and no matter how busy you are, how many sports or activities your children participate in, how many games you attend, how many committees you serve on, your children grow up. And childhood ends. I am speaking from the knowledge given to me from friends and family, and have talked about this with many parents whose children were all part of the glorification of busy. More often than not, they have regrets. They regret the fact that their children's childhoods were spent running from practice to practice, game to game, all in a blur of activity. And in the end, their children grew up. The thing they missed most? They missed the family time, the moments of simply being together with their kids, sitting around the dinner table, taking a walk after dinner, playing a game of kickball in the yard.

What is so wrong with allowing kids to play outside after school, riding bikes, playing chase, catching bugs, shooting hoops, just for fun? What happened to allowing our children a childhood that consisted of playing outside, washing up, and sitting down to dinner at the family table? Unscheduled activities lead to freedom and imagination, and that is as important as schedule and competition. Society is producing a generation of youths who cannot relax and fill time with fun, unscheduled activities, a generation that does not value family and peaceful, reflective time spent with loved ones.

I don't expect everyone to agree with me. Some families are naturally active. Asking them to stop activities would be the equivalent of asking me to hike the mountains every weekend. That is not going to happen! What I'm suggesting is that we make an effort to preserve the sanctity of family. We must allow our families to come first, before sports and activities and parties and practices and craziness and running around. I am hoping that we can enable our children to find comfort in the quiet, unscheduled, peaceful routine of family life. How can we do that? Simple. Eat dinner together. Take walks together. Play games together. Watch television together. Bake cookies together. Laugh together.

Be together in moments of peace. These are the moments our children will tuck into their souls and pull out years from now. These are the moments they will recreate with their children someday.

Stop the glorification of busy. Allow yourself to take a stand. Say no to society. Say yes to your family. And you will find real peace, peace not only in your home but also in your heart. How do I know this? We have done it. We have found it. And it is good.

Changes

August 28, 2014

I find comfort in routine, in the predictable flow of our daily lives. Lately, however, we experienced changes in our lives. Some changes are significant, like the passing of my dear father just six months ago, and affect us on a deep level, forcing us to create a new normal while mourning the one we leave behind. Some changes are minor, like switching doctors because our favorite relocated, switching parishes to one closer to our home, or friends and neighbors moving away from our small neighborhood, leaving only memories of neighbor kids knocking on the door asking if Peyton and Rhett can come out and play. These changes force me to move out of my comfortable world. This is a challenge for me, but also a reminder that life is all about transitions. And as hard as it is, I must embrace the change and be thankful for the chance to experience it, while holding on to the memories left behind.

Contentment

February 12, 2015

This morning I was playing a game of Disney Princess Memory with Flynn, and I was struck by a genuine feeling of contentment. This was followed by an overwhelming sense of gratitude. I felt so thankful to be there at that moment, in my home, with my family. I was aware of the blessings I had and wanted nothing more.

I am thankful for that moment. It served as a reminder to me of how very blessed I am. We live in a world where we are always told that more is better. That we need more...more money, more clothes, more electronic devices, more data. We are bombarded with images of extravagant places we need to visit, and are encouraged to be as busy as we can with numerous extracurricular activities for our children.

All of this comes at the expense of something. Something I cherish. Something I was reminded of this morning as I sat with my ever-growing, ever-changing, little girl. It comes at the expense of just BEING...being present, being in the moment, being content with what we are blessed to have; waking every morning in a home with those we love. And needing or wanting nothing more.

Her Photo Album

February 26, 2015

Recently, my mother asked me to go through her photo albums and scrapbooks for her. She wants to share the photos of her life and family with her daughters and feels overwhelmed by the task. I told her I would be happy to and assured her that I would take great care in going through the photos documenting her amazing life.

Each day, I sit at the table and sort through a lifetime of memories, baby pictures, family gatherings, high school dances. I study random snapshots from an everyday life lived years ago in a different time and place. Many of the photos are black and white, some yellowed with age. There are photos of people my mother talks about with love, people who were a part of her life; her parents, grandparents, sister, brothers, and friends. There are photos of my father and her smiling before they headed out to the prom. And I find I am fascinated by these faces and events. So much that I'm cherishing the time spent on actually looking at and seeing the people who meant so much to my mother and father. Their lives were full of people and places long before they were parents and grandparents. And these pictures tell that story. I want to be sure their stories aren't lost. Ever.

And so I carefully remove the pictures from the albums. As I do, I think about the people in each one. I think about what I know about their lives. And how much I don't. I make piles — one for myself and one for each of my sisters. I make an extra pile. Someday I will sit down with my mother and listen as she tells me about each one. I will make notes on the back so that I can share the stories of these amazing people with my sisters and my children. These are people who were a part of my parents' lives. And a part of mine and my children. Their lives and stories should not be confined to pages in an album. They should be remembered and displayed and shared. Just as I hope our photographs will be, someday, in a different place and time.

Learning Through Play

March 26, 2015

Today I thought about how very much our children learn from us. Not necessarily the things we consciously teach them, but rather about the things they learn from us by simply watching. Children learn how to live through daily observation of their parents and caregivers. They learn how to love, work, play, laugh, and interact. They learn how to become wives and husbands and fathers and mothers through our actions. What a tremendous responsibility! But what an honor as well.

What made my mind go to this profound place today? Well, just yesterday Flynn asked me to help her create a daily schedule for her babydoll. She brought me a piece of paper and a pen and asked me to write the words she said. Then she proceeded to dictate her To-Do list for today. You see, she was going to be the Mommy today. And she wanted to compile a list of things to accomplish. As she spoke, and as I wrote, I realized that these are the things she sees me doing daily. Today, when she woke, she asked me what time it was. Nine o'clock was her baby's bath time. And at nine sharp we gave her baby a (pretend) bath. I watched in amazement as she recreated every step I complete when I bathe and help her dress. Then we got breakfast. She made me coffee in her kitchen center. And we checked off her list. At first glance, it seems like a simple game of playing house. But beyond that, I believe it was an opportunity for a little girl to learn how to love and care for others, whilst acquiring the skills and foster the emotions necessary for later in life. I am grateful for days like these. I am thankful I can play dolls again with my daughter. But I am also grateful to Flynn for the reminder that my children learn from me. Even when I don't know I'm teaching.

Firsts

April 27, 2015

Years ago, when I was pregnant with my Madison, I received a milestone calendar to mark the important dates of her first year: her first smile, her first tooth, the first time she rolled over, and the first steps she took. I was vigilant about anticipating these significant moments in my baby's life and was thrilled every time I got to document one on her calendar.

Lately, as my baby approaches Kindergarten, I'm thinking less about the firsts and more about the lasts. The lasts sneak up on us, and we often don't even know they've occurred until afterward. A few weeks ago, when Flynn took my hand as I walked to Communion at Mass instead of lifting her arms to be picked up, it hit me. I had carried a baby in church for the last time. And I hadn't even known it.

When Madison was little and still in her crib, we had her big girl bed all ready for her. One day she stated she wanted to sleep in it. As excited as I was for her, I cried myself to sleep that night. That very morning, I had walked into her nursery and saw her smiling face and watched her jump up and down holding the crib rail that she had chewed on while teething. I had lifted her out of that crib for the last time. And I hadn't even known it.

When Peyton was little, every morning while Rhett napped and Madison was at school, she and I had coffee and toast. We would sit together in a big chair. She had milk, and I had coffee. We shared toast, and she would always take the last sip of my coffee. One day, I got up from that chair and put that coffee cup away for the last time. And I hadn't even known it.

When Rhett was a baby, he had a favorite book. It was called Big Farm Tractor. Every single day, we snuggled in the rocker in his room and read that book before his afternoon nap. One day I closed that book and set it down. I tucked my little boy into his bed for his nap for the last time. And I hadn't even known it.

I didn't know when I changed a diaper, bought formula, gave a bubble bath, carried a baby up the stairs or pushed one in a stroller that it would be the last time I would do it. I didn't know it. And I am so thankful for that. I don't think my heart would be able to stand knowing that those simple moments of mothering were ending. As much as I realize that a large part of mothering means letting go, I still resist and mourn change. As much as I anticipate the firsts, I dread the lasts. I long to hang onto childhood. It's beautiful and safe and cozy. But as my dear friend Tara reminded me, these last moments can be sweet too. And I realize that the lasts mean something else. They signify new firsts.

The last time my Flynn had me carry her in church meant that the next week she would walk herself. And she was so proud to do so. The last time I drove Madison to work meant the next time she would drive herself. And she was thrilled to do so. Mothering is indeed letting go. And learning to embrace it. One last at a time.

Dr. Seuss

June 8, 2015

Years ago, when Madison was a newborn, I received a card in the mail offering membership to a Dr. Seuss book club. This was long before the days of internet shopping and Amazon. I was excited to join and looked forward every few months to receiving a brand-new Dr. Seuss book in the mail. I couldn't wait to begin reading to my baby, and I remember sitting on the couch with a then two-month-old baby reading Hop on Pop and Go, Dog, Go!

Madison grew to LOVE those books, which I carefully stored first in a basket and then on a shelf. We read them over and over and over. Her favorite was Dr. Seuss's ABC. I swear I read that book over a thousand times. As Madison outgrew those particular books, Peyton and Rhett came along, and we enjoyed them all over again. I remember being excited every time we read them.

Gradually my three littles grew, and those precious books took their spot on our children's bookshelf. Years went by before our sweet little Flynn came along. Flynn's childhood is quite different. She was born after the advent of the internet and ABC Mouse and iPad games. We still read books, of course. But books are now readily available through Amazon, and we are enjoying new favorites, like her never-ending collection of Llama Llama books. Last week, however, she discovered a collection of books on the shelf. And she has carried them around for days. She asks to read them over and over and over. And my heart is happy to do so! Each time I read one, I am transported back in time in my heart and mind. I am reading the same words to my littlest that I did all those years ago to my older three. I am watching her enjoy and savor every page just as they did when we snuggled together on a different couch in a different house.

Years pass. Children grow. Things change. Or do they? I still love to read those precious books, and my children still love to listen. I know someday I will put them back on the shelf for good as my baby outgrows them. But I also know that one day, hopefully, I will pull them off again and snuggle on my couch with a new generation of babies, my grandchildren. And I will open a book and begin again.

Do Your Own Thing

July 20, 2015

We don't spend our summer days at the pool. We don't spend our summer evenings at the ball field.

We do our own thing. And that's quite alright. If there's something I have learned over my almost nineteen blessed years of mothering, it's that it's okay to do your own thing, and what makes you and your family happy.

What makes you happy may not always be the norm. It may not always be what everyone else is doing. And that's alright. I haven't always felt so confident about this. Turning forty a few years ago, however, allowed me the freedom to stop worrying. To stop worrying about pleasing others and find comfort in the fact that by doing what we enjoy, our family may be different, but not wrong.

Young mothers, do what you want. Live YOUR life. Find joy in the things that make you happy. Respect the fact that others may have different interests and hobbies. Refrain from judging others based on your differences. Don't compare yourself or your parenting to anyone else. No one knows your family better than you.

If you ever find yourself feeling pressured or inadequate or uncertain, remember this. No one knows your heart or your family, your strengths or your challenges, your interests, or your dreams more than you. No one else knows what makes your family happy. You may do things differently, and you may not be the norm. And you know what? That's honestly quite alright.

Kids In The Kitchen

April 25, 2016

From the time they were little, my children joined me in the kitchen. At first, it was because I enjoyed their company. And when I mean at first, I mean a babbling baby in a bouncy seat. Gradually, the bouncy seat was replaced by a highchair, and then a booster, until finally, little legs up on a stool. Without realizing, I bestowed a passion and an ability for cooking and baking upon my children.

One of my fondest memories is Peyton and Rhett perched on their yellow Little Tikes chairs smack dab in front of the oven for an entire 30 minutes waiting for the brownies they mixed up to bake. Another is Peyton, not yet four, mixing up the incredible Chocolate Chip Pumpkin Bread she still makes today. Those moments with my children as littles in the kitchen may be gone, but the result of that precious time spent together is witnessed here every day.

Madison, Peyton, and Rhett show ability beyond their ages in the cooking and baking department. Peyton and Madison each currently select a night during the week to plan and prepare a meal. Peyton's is almost always Japanese, while Madison introduces us to new things like pesto on pasta. Peyton is my master baker. She makes pies, cakes, cookies, and brownies.

So, young mothers, bring your children into the kitchen with you. Show them how to mix with a spoon. Let them crack an egg. Show them how to plan a meal, and how to set the table. You will make memories to store in your heart. You will also reap the benefits years down the road as you sit and watch your children prepare a delicious dinner and a fantastic dessert. I still clean up after them a bit; I kind of like my kitchen just so.

In Their Own Time

August 15, 2016

A few months ago, we attended a birthday party for Flynn's friend. He is a sweet little guy. While Flynn homeschools, he attends Kindergarten in a small public school. When it came time to open the presents, her little friend carefully removed every card and read each aloud. I was impressed and very happy for him! At the same time, a seed of doubt popped into my mind. Flynn was nowhere near that place in her reading. Was I doing it wrong? Was I hindering her ability? But just as quickly, a complete sense of calm came over me. I reminded myself of something I had learned through twenty years of parenting my four little blessings. And I yanked out that seed of doubt before it ever had a chance to grow.

In my experience, children will do most things in their own time. Rolling over, crawling, walking, tying shoes, buttoning coats, reading words, and then books. All I need to do is patiently present and demonstrate and sit back and watch them try. I can lend assistance and offer praise when necessary. No panicking or self-doubt required.

Yesterday, Flynn came to me with a book, one I had read to her many, many times. And guess what? She asked if she could read it to me. So, we cuddled on the couch, and my little girl read. She read and giggled and sounded out words. She reread it at night to the family. And she did wonderfully. Best of all, she did it in her own time.

Children will do most things in their own time. Comparing, panicking and reevaluating are merely wastes of our precious time with our littles. Of course, some instances of a child meeting certain milestones may require medical advice. For the most part, however, children do things in their own time. So relax and enjoy watching as your child grows before your very eyes.

Perspective And Peace

September 12, 2016

I will never be a size four again. For my entire youth and early adulthood, I was tiny. Really tiny. Now, not so much. But I am comforted by the fact that this body nurtured and brought four beautiful, blessed babies into this world. And every single way it is different is more than worth it. Now, a few pounds heavier, I am thankful for where I am with this body of mine. I eat what I want. In moderation, of course. Now I have to think about cholesterol! But I don't sweat the desserts I so enjoy.

I will most likely never push a baby of mine in a stroller again. Or open the nursery door to see my baby peeking out from the crib with that "just woke up" smile. I won't buy diapers or wipes or Gerber Rice cereal. I won't have that baby to sit with me while everyone else rides the big rides at the park. I am almost forty-seven years old, and my baby days are more than likely behind me. But I had baby days! I was blessed to bring four new souls home from the hospital. I am honored to be a part of their lives and watch as each baby grows and changes into the individual God created each to be. And so I embrace each new stage with excitement and wonder, mixed with a twinge of sadness.

I will never hold my Dad's hand again. I will never hear his voice on the other end of the phone. I won't see that smile or hear that laugh, or see those eyes light up ever again. I won't listen to him call me his "Little Buddy" or invite him up for Chicken Cacciatore ever again. I won't smell his baby powder or bring him coffee and donuts. I won't ever see him sitting on my couch holding my mother's hand. This is a tough one. One I will always struggle with. But I force myself to look at it this way: Dad is in Heaven. He is happier, healthier, and holier than he ever was here. And as much as I miss him every single day, I am comforted by that fact. And by the fact that he lives on in things he taught me, the love he shared, and in my son, who resembles him more and more each day. And of course, I will see him again one day. That fact gives me peace.

I Want My Kids To Know

February 13, 2017

Do you remember the days before Google, when we had to think about how and where to look for the information we needed? Technology is wonderful. It brings the world to our fingertips. Part of me worries, however, about the things our children will never have to do and the things they will never have to learn. While I embrace all this fantastic new technology, I also cling to certain parts of the past that I feel should not be lost. And that is why I want my kids to know a few things I think shouldn't be forgotten.

I want them to know how to look up names in a phone book. Perhaps the day is near that these books will be obsolete, but I still think kids should know the essential skill of looking things up using alphabetical order. Searching for information rather than having it magically appear increases the possibility of actual retention.

I want them to know how to make and receive a phone call. Maybe we won't be using phones as much as or in the same way as in the past, but I believe the basic principles of good manners should remain. Not to mention an engaging conversation is much more enjoyable than an impersonal text.

I want my children to know how to write a note and a thank you card with actual paper and pen. I hope and pray this simple gesture isn't lost amid the fast-paced world of texts, Facebook, and Instagram that dominates our world today. It is so important to me that my children realize how much people appreciate and enjoy an actual acknowledgment of a kind deed. I fear that in this age of instant gratification, young people lose the ability to appreciate things fully. The simple gesture of writing a thank you note ensures that my children appreciate the kindness of others.

I want my kids to know what it feels like to hold a book in their hands. Ebooks are convenient, but nothing can replace the feeling of holding an actual book in your hands, of knowing that inside the cover, words arranged on pieces of well-worn pages await you, and an adventure is about to begin.

I also want my children to know how to play. Our world is filled with noise and fast-paced electronic games with flashing lights and sounds. Our children are surrounded by high tech phones, game systems, and computers. While all these are fun and engaging, something is missing. I want my children to know the quiet thoughtfulness and pure enjoyment that sitting and playing a classic game brings to families.

Finally, I want my children to know how to make homemade pasta sauce. I mean the kind that simmers on the stove all day long, the kind my grandmother taught my father to make because that's something that should never be lost.

Swing Sets

May 1, 2017

Swing sets. Few things evoke such strong childhood memories. I remember our swing set. It was on the side of our back yard. I remember many hours spent on that metal swing, going so high the legs would come up out of the ground. I can still remember how it felt to lean back so far my bare feet seemed to touch the clouds.

I knew that when I became a mother, I would have a swing set in my backyard. We moved into our home soon after Madison turned one, and the first thing I did was get a swing set. Not a fancy wooden one with three levels and a telephone. Just a regular metal one, like I had as a kid. That swing set did not disappoint. I spent hours upon hours pushing my Madison, first in a baby swing, then on her big girl swing, and eventually watching as she and her friend Jeffrey played on the glider.

Peyton loved the swing. I remember pushing her over and over and over. We played the same game every time. She would ask me what holiday was next. After I told her, she would say, "And then what, Mommy?" It went on until we got through the whole year. Rhett inherited the baby swing once he was old enough to join us. I look back now on those days as some of the happiest days of my life.

I was sad to leave that old metal swing set behind when we moved to a new house several years later. It held so many memories. As soon as our new yard was ready, we put in a new swing set. Because we had three young children, we opted for a wooden one this time, with a fort and a slide as well. Our neighbors all had similar ones in their yards, and the kids spent many hours playing on the swings, riding bikes from yard to yard.

Hot summer afternoons. Cool autumn evenings. Sunny winter days. And dewy spring mornings. The swing set was a constant in our lives. As the years passed, the wooden swing sets slowly disappeared from our neighbors' yards. As kids grew, they sat empty. They were disassembled and removed. I couldn't imagine taking ours down, even though the kids continued to grow. Fortunately, God blessed us with our sweet little Flynn, and the baby swing went back up again. And I began again. Pushing a little on a swing, watching as she learns to swing herself. Watching my older kids swing with her, capturing moments of their childhoods once again.

Easter morning was one of the very first days it was nice enough to be outside. Flynn was the first one ready, and I wasn't surprised that she asked to swing. So swing she did in her Easter dress and her brand-new sandals. Moments like these pass so very quickly. Soon enough, those swings will be empty, moving only in the breeze. But not just yet.

Grace

June 5, 2017

Nine years ago, I was a young mother, blessed beyond measure with three healthy, beautiful babies. While none of our pregnancies came easily, I held on to the hope of having just one more. It wasn't happening, and Steve and I were beginning to think about possible adoption, when one day after picking the kids up from school, I began to feel tremendous pain. Steve eventually talked me into going to my doctor, who immediately admitted me to the hospital. At this time, our children were eleven, seven, and five. My sister and mother came to stay with the kids while Steve waited with me at the hospital. Finally, with the help of medication, my pain subsided, and my doctor came in to tell us that I was pregnant! It was very early on, and he had some concerns. I will always remember how he sat down and spoke with me, rather than at me, and explained that he was a doctor, not God, and only God knew what would happen to this new little soul.

Later that evening, after Steve had left to go home to our little ones, I prayed until I fell asleep. I dreamt the baby was a little girl, and when I awoke, I decided to call her Grace. Steve arrived, and while we talked, he told me that he too felt the baby was a girl, and so she became our little Grace. I was discharged after a few days, and while my HCG levels were not rising, I held out hope. My doctor released me with strict instructions to rest and told me to call him when the bleeding started. It didn't hit me until I was home. He said when, not if, the bleeding started.

Steve and I decided then we wouldn't share the news of this baby with our children. I realize this is not a decision everyone would make. For us, it was the right one. Our children wanted a baby as badly as we did. They prayed for a new baby all the time. We couldn't explain this situation to them when it was so raw to us. And they were still so young.

Eventually, I did experience the heart-wrenching ache of losing a baby. I suffered a miscarriage and spent the following week having my blood tested to watch the HCG levels diminish. It was the most emotionally, physically, and mentally difficult period of my life. But my faith carried me through that dark time. And God let me know that our Grace was with God, and we would be reunited with her someday.

I will never forget the ways that our sweet Grace reached across eternity to let us know she was happy and safe and at home with God. The first time it happened was shortly after our loss. I was bathing Rhett, and suddenly he looked right at me. Out of the blue, he said, "Mom, I gave my guardian angel a name. I named her Grace." I will never forget the feeling of our baby letting me know that she would always be with us. I felt her. I knew. I just knew.

A few weeks later, Steve and I went to the gift shop at the convent here in town. We were looking for something that would keep our little Grace near to us and a part of our family. The sweet little nun helped us pick out the perfect piece, and as we were leaving, she smiled and told us that God would bless us again very soon. I felt a sense of peace come over me when she spoke those words, and I clung to them during the difficult months that followed.

Later that year, on the day our little Grace was due to be born, Steve took me out for the day. We went to lunch at Red Lobster, and yet again, I experienced the goodness of God. After we were seated, our waitress made her way over to our table. She was so happy and approached our table smiling. Before she said a word, I knew. I just knew. She smiled again and said hello. Her name? Grace.

Finally, when we arrived home that day, I saw that we had received a letter from our friend Father Leon. On the back of the envelope, he had placed a sticker. The sticker was of a young girl with long brown hair. She had angel wings. I knew once more. It was my Grace.

I am so thankful for those messages from God. Although this is a very personal part of our lives, I share it to give anyone who is in the same situation hope and peace; hope for the future and peace in knowing that God hears all prayers, and answers them in His own way, in His own time.

A year and a half or so after we lost our Grace and were comforted by a sweet nun in her gift shop, we welcomed our surprise blessing, our Flynn Grace. I am convinced that our precious Flynn was sent here for us by not only God but also by her sister Grace, as a sign that God does indeed hear all prayers. Our family is proof of that.

Kindness Matters

October 2, 2017

As I sat in the waiting room at the orthodontist this morning, I found myself witnessing an all too familiar scene. A young girl was happily chatting to herself about the new toothbrush and bag of goodies she received, yet each time she spoke, her older brother criticized and mocked her quite rudely. Meanwhile, their mother sat right between them, either oblivious or unconcerned.

Unfortunately, I see this kind of behavior from both children and adults so often, I'm almost immune. Almost. I refuse to admit that rude, disrespectful, inconsiderate behavior is the new normal for our society today. I don't want it to be. I expect more from people, especially parents. Why parents? The fact is, as parents, we are charged with raising our children to be kind, empathetic, respectable members of society. How can we do that when so many adults are modeling the exact opposite behavior in front of their children?

This past summer on our family vacation, my children and husband witnessed a grown man berating a server over whether a jar of seasoning was crushed garlic or not. This man was outright bullying an employee in front of many people, adults and children alike. Another time, I stood next to an older man who belittled a chef because he didn't add enough cheese to his omelet. Lastly, that same day, I watched as a mother asked her young child what she wanted to eat, only to chastise her for saying pizza when the mother wanted something else. She grabbed the little girl and ignored her confused face as she pulled her away.

My husband and I used each of these incidents as an opportunity to teach our children the importance of a simple human virtue: kindness. We try to instill in our children a sense of empathy and respect for others. We want them to see that other people are just as deserving of a kind word or a smile as they are. And we expect them to treat them that way. Your children don't just magically see others deserving of a kind word or smile. As parents, we must teach them and remember to model the appropriate behavior to instill a desire in them to do the same.

For example, last night, my son and I were in the drive-thru of our favorite fast food restaurant. Yes, we eat fast food. Too much, I'm sure. Anyway, we waited a long time for our food, and when the young girl at the window went to hand the box to us, the bottom fell out, and everything fell onto the floor. The poor girl froze in fear. My heart broke for her as her manager came over. It was clear the manager was looking to me to see how to proceed. I smiled and told the young girl that it was fine! Things like that happen to me all the time. I offered to pull ahead and wait. When she returned with our fresh food a few minutes later, she was almost in tears. I reassured her again that it was not a problem. And she was smiling before we left.

Another time, in the same drive-thru, a young girl was short with me when I asked her a question. I smiled and said nothing. As we waited for our food, I remarked to my children that you never know what another person is going through at any given moment. Maybe she was having a bad day? Perhaps she didn't feel well? Sure enough, when she returned, she was very apologetic and told me she was having a tough day. I assured her I have those days too. And not to worry about it at all.

Both of these incidents were opportunities to teach not only my children but also the young women that kindness matters. I was able to demonstrate that feeling empathy and having respect for others is a necessary social skill in our world today. At least it should be. Before you begin to think I'm Mary Poppins, Ma Ingalls, and Mother of the Year all rolled in one; I assure you I am not always successful in modeling appropriate behavior. I am human, after all. My children are not always perfectly behaved. They're human too. Yet we try. We respect. We talk kindly to others. We smile. We treat others as we want to be treated.

And you know what? Others notice. And appreciate it. More than once, people we meet remark that our family is kind and unique. They say they don't meet people like our family every day. Do I say this to boast? Not at all. I am way too paranoid for that. I say this as an affirmation that kindness matters. People notice. And they appreciate it. And they, in turn, may show others the same kindness. Wouldn't that be nice?

I sound preachy, I know. I am merely tired of unkind people. Am I a Pollyanna? A Holly Hobby? You bet. Do I wish the world was all rainbows and unicorns? Not at all. Do I want my children to grow up in a world filled with more kindness and less rudeness? You bet. So parents, let's put down the phones and laptops and television remotes and do what we are here to do, raise our children to know this one simple thing, kindness matters.

Roles Reverse

February 5, 2018

I was sitting at my kitchen table a few days ago, writing out bills for my mother. As I was signing them, I suddenly stopped and thought about how our lives unfold, and our roles reverse. It's funny, isn't it? How we can go along, day by day, living our lives until suddenly, something random causes us to stop and reflect on a much bigger picture. Like the way our mothers care for us for so many years, and if we are blessed, someday we have the chance to care for them in return.

As I wrote out her bills that day, I thought about how many times my dear mother had written out and signed things for me. I thought about her being a young mother filling out permission slips for field trips and signing checks for majorette boots and batons. I thought about how many times she sat at the kitchen table signing report cards and health forms.

Today, as I carefully filled my mother's pill case for the week, I thought about how years ago, she had opened the Bayer Baby Aspirin bottle and counted out pills for me. I thought about how my mom gave me Flintstone Vitamins every morning and Castoria every Saturday night.

My mom stayed with us this weekend, and last night I pulled the comforter down and smoothed out the sheets on her bed. I thought about all the times my mom had changed the sheets on my bed and how many times she had tucked me in. Those memories so often make me wish I were back there, in my mom and dad's house, watching my mom write out bills, and fix my bedsheets. They also make me realize how very blessed I am to be able to do these small acts of love for my mother. I am blessed to have had her nurture me and love me and care for me all these years. I am thankful that I can do these small things in return. And I am blessed that I am but one link in this unending chain of mothers and daughters in this amazing thing called life.

Give Simple A Try

March 12, 2018

Scrolling through Pinterest one day, I wondered just what happened to simplicity. With apologies to all who search Pinterest for the most creative and complex treats for their kids, I'm going to say that enough is enough. Moms, go easy on yourself. Simple is better, trust me.

As a second grade teacher many years ago, I saw the many snacks and treats my students brought for parties. I witnessed the elaborate, individually decorated cupcakes adorned with unwrapped candies. I also saw the prepackaged cupcakes in the plastic wrappers. I specifically remember one thing very clearly. My students would look at and pick apart the messy, unwrapped cupcakes that an ambitious mom labored over. They would set them aside, and then they rip open the plastic and eat the store bought treats as fast as they could!

In a world where competition often overshadows common sense, it's easy to feel pressured to spend hours using homemade icing to glue tiny cookies onto a Twinkie. I am here to tell you; you don't have to do that! Buy a box of cupcakes, cookies or fruit cups and call it a day. Spend the time you save playing a game with your children or perhaps taking a walk. After all, who do we moms need to impress? The other mothers? The teachers? Or our children, who will remember the time spent laughing with us as we watched a movie together way longer than those elaborate marshmallow-covered sheep cookies? A simple cupcake and a cup of Kool-aid, the party treats of the 1970s. That's what we enjoyed. Go easy on yourself. And give simple a try.

Trust

June 20, 2018

When Madison returned to Denmark in May, she left her beautiful little orchid behind. She asked Flynn to take care of it for her. Although Flynn had never cared for a plant before, she agreed in a heartbeat. And so Madison left her very special orchid in her little sister's hands.

Madison placed her trust in Flynn to care for and nurture her little flower. As for Flynn, she continued to demonstrate a good amount of faith and perseverance. She had faith that even though she had no idea how to care for the little plant, she could do her very best by following the directions Madison gave her. And Flynn most certainly demonstrated perseverance as she waited for some sign that her faith and hard work would come to fruition. She continued to water and watch and wait until one day, a tiny bud appeared. Then finally, the beautiful white flower bloomed. The joy and excitement in her little voice as she told Madison all about it is something I will remember forever.

I could take a lesson from these two young people. What if I tried harder to stop analyzing and worrying and instead, trusted that the God who cares for me would either protect me from the things I worry about or help me through whatever it is I fear? What if I had more faith and perseverance in my prayer life? Perhaps I would find that I too would be filled with joy. And that peace would replace the anxious pieces of my soul.

Routine

July 11, 2018

Routine. Something I cling to like a life preserver in the middle of a storm. I need it. My children need it. Years ago, when I was teaching sweet second graders, I began every morning by sharing our schedule for the day. Kids need structure and thrive when they know what comes next. I'm the same way. I function best when I follow a routine. As I grow older, I'm finding my routine is less structured. But it's still routine. And it works for me!

Every morning after Steve and I have our coffee and tea, and as he gets ready for work, I tidy the kitchen and throw a load of laundry in the washer. I make the bed, smooth the comforter, and arrange the pillows. Then I fold up any blankets and straighten the cushions on the sofa. During these beautiful summer months, I also head out to the deck and check the plants. I like to sweep the deck too and arrange the furniture. Usually, by this time, the kids are still asleep, and Steve has headed off to work. I either exercise or hop in the shower. Sometimes I even hop back into bed.

Every evening, after dinner, I help the kids with the

kitchen. The kids do most of the cooking now, so I usually just clean up. They all head outside and go for a walk or play a game of Four Square together. I love that they have so much fun together. Standing at the sink, listening to the laughter coming from the yard, reminds me that I'm blessed to be living the life I dreamed. After I wipe every surface and sweep the floor, I turn out the lights and light the candle. Then I close the blinds and turn on some lamps. I tidy the sofa and fold any blankets, even though I know soon enough we'll be using them while we gather together for our evening television time. My life is simple, I know. Simple. And happy.

Caring And Creating Cozy

August 6, 2018

I often write about the importance of slowing down and making time for myself each day. How do I accomplish this in our chaotic, fast-paced world where society dictates that busy is better? How do I nourish my soul to be able to bring peace and calm to my home and family? Well, my schedule constantly changes and evolves depending on which season of life I am in, but I continue to make time each day for calm and peace and coffee. I began to create this particular time when I was a young mother who decided one day to pour a cup of coffee and snuggle in a chair as her sweet baby girl napped each afternoon.

When neighbors called and invited us to the park or the pool, I politely declined. My children needed a schedule, and I needed it too. More important than keeping up with all the chaos outside and the ever-present need for busyness was my desire to create a place of comfort, stability, and warmth for my family. By caring for myself a little each day, I was able to do just that. As more babies came along and children grew, I continued to keep that particular time during each day as an anchor for calm, peace, and rest. And I still do to this day. My children often join me now, cozy with coffee, tea, or milk, taking a few moments in the middle of our day to rest and be together.

In addition to my afternoon coffee, I also make sure to spend some time each morning doing something for myself. When the children were little, that may have meant a shower and a ponytail before they woke up! These days, I have teenagers who tend to sleep quite late. This allows for a morning routine that includes some exercise like walking or yoga. I am loving the peace and calm yoga brings. Madison and I light a candle and spend ten to fifteen minutes with a yoga video she finds on YouTube. Am I an expert? Not even close. Do I get dressed up and go to the gym in perfect workout clothes? No way. I am here to tell you it is perfectly acceptable to do yoga in mismatched pajamas and with severe bedhead.

Candles are a great way to bring peace and warmth into your home. It is incredible the amount of cozy a simple candle can bring to a home. If you can't burn candles, or would rather not, battery operated candles with timers are a great option that I also enjoy. Every evening, I turn the lights down, light a candle, and pull out the throw blankets. Blankets are the perfect way to encourage cozy in your home. I have them everywhere! Soft throw blankets lying around make our home more inviting to family members and guests.

Taking time for yourself, sipping coffee, burning candles, saying no to outside distractions, snuggling in cozy throws, these are all ways to make your home and life more peaceful.

Calmer. More centered. One more essential thing? Make your family your priority. Say no to unnecessary meetings, sports events, projects, parties, and commitments that draw you away from the comfort of your home and create stress and chaos as you try to balance it all. This enables you to maintain a warm, cozy, loving home for your family. A place of calm, stability, and peace that serves as a haven for your loved ones in this otherwise hectic and demanding world.

The Doorway To Motherhood

August 20, 2018

As I begin planning the wedding of my oldest child, I find myself reflecting on this blessed gift of motherhood. My children are now twenty-one, eighteen, sixteen, and eight, and as the years pass, the struggle my husband and I faced to build our family seems so distant I have to remind myself of the pain and agony of infertility. I search my mind and soul for a specific memory of those days, months, and years I longed to be a mommy.

Being told by different doctors that I would have a minimal chance of ever having a child of my own without medical intervention was devastating and heart-wrenching. Yet, here I am with four blessed children here on Earth, and one holy soul in Heaven. Each one of our babies came after years of waiting and praying and hoping. Because of this, I never want to take this vocation of motherhood for granted. I want to remember how I felt as I struggled to make sense of the heartbreak of infertility.

I imagined my dream of motherhood existing behind a large, wooden door. Women enter this door in many different ways. Some women, when ready, knock on the beautiful wooden door, and it opens right away. I am so happy for these women, who step inside and begin their life-changing journey as mothers immediately. For some women, the wait between that first tentative tap on the door and gaining entry is a bit longer. They may look around a bit outside as they wait patiently for the door to open, and when it does, they happily step inside. Some women, myself included, knock and knock and knock on that door until our knuckles bleed. The door creaks open, and quickly shuts again before we can enter as the agony of miscarriage is realized.

I remember thinking of myself and many other women, pounding on that door until we fell to our knees, sobbing at the thought of being locked out of our dream of motherhood. I remember thinking that it seemed so unfair. Some women didn't even have to knock. The door to mothering seemed to open for them effortlessly. Infertility is a lonely place, and try as one might, it is hard to continually celebrate the joys of others as you continue to beg for a chance to enter the realm of motherhood yourself.

Some women eventually cease knocking and slowly look around. These blessed women see through their tears that other doors exist nearby. And after much discernment, they venture over to these different doors and are welcomed inside. They embrace their vocation of adoption and foster care and bless so many children as they are blessed themselves.

After years of trying, I finally gained entry into the beautiful and blessed world of mothering through the main door. Once inside, I immersed myself in the joy and beauty of this place that I had dreamed of my entire life. I found motherhood to be precisely what I hoped. It was a continuous stream of loving moments: rocking swaddled babies, smelling Baby Magic on tiny foreheads as I slipped wiggly arms and legs into soft little outfits with small snaps up the middle, singing ABC songs, first pairs of tiny baby shoes, bibs and blankets in the wash, frosted cupcakes, swimming lessons, and Christmas trees. I spent years surrounded by Max and Ruby and Little Bear on television, scooters and training wheels in the yard, and Barbies and Matchbox Cars on the carpet. Time passed, as those sweet baby days were replaced with preschool pick up, and then finally school days and part-time jobs.

I began to look around my cozy little world and suddenly realized I was closer to the exit than I was the entrance. And I didn't feel ready to leave. I wanted to stay just a little longer in this safe and unique cocoon I'd created. The door to the next room seemed to beckon me, and just as I was about to open it and walk through and begin the next chapter of my life, I glanced back and saw my blessed little Flynn. I was blessed with one more soul and with one more chance to do it all again! I turned and closed that door leading out, and ran back to savor the joys of childhood once more.

As I near my twenty-second year of motherhood, I realize that what everyone tells you is correct. The days, months, and years pass quickly. The baby I rocked yesterday will become a wife very soon. The little girl with the short brown hair and Blue's Clues shirt and the little boy who brought trucks and baseballs into my home are learning to drive now. And the special little gift of our baby girl is now starting third grade. Thankfully, the vocation of motherhood never ends. While I pray my years of mothering will result in four happy, healthy, responsible adults, I know that will mean closing one of the many doors of motherhood, leaving these precious days of children at home behind. I am and will always be tremendously thankful for the gift of motherhood and the memories I will hold in my heart forever. I also imagine that somewhere down the hall lies another door. Someday, I pray that door will open for me, and I will be greeted by little ones that run to me and call me Grandma.

Change

November 28, 2018

Christmas comes every December. We wait for it, dream about it, and prepare for it. Recently, I realized that although Christmas comes every year, I don't have to prepare our family to celebrate it the same way. We grow and change. Our lives and family circumstances evolve. It's alright to change the way we enjoy this special time of year, while still keeping our focus on what is important.

As a young mother of little children, I found it necessary to schedule our December in a very particular way. I planned the shopping, wrapping, baking, Santa visiting, and picture taking well in advance. I even made a handwritten schedule complete with dates and events and little festive stickers. And that worked for us until it didn't.

Now, as a mother of older children, our focus remains the same: keeping December centered on our family and the cozy time we spend together preparing for the most blessed Christmas Day. My approach, however, has changed. Gone are the detailed lists and scheduled events. We are much more relaxed now, as we focus on our little family and spending these precious days together.

What do December days look like around here? Because they seem to pass so quickly, I plan on spending them here in our cozy home, sipping coffee and cocoa from Santa mugs, playing Christmas games, listening to classical Christmas music and watching our favorite Christmas movies. We will venture out to do some local Christmas shopping and to Mass, and we do have a special wedding shower for a special bride to be! Other than that, we will be right here. Safe and sound. Together.

Be In The Moment

January 23, 2019

Years ago, shortly before Madison was born, Steve and I purchased our very first camcorder. It was large and bulky and came in a big black bag. Every once in a while, we lugged it out and taped our sweet new baby playing, crawling or smiling. As the years passed, we added new members to our family, and we continued to use the camcorder to record the special and sometimes ordinary events of our lives.

Gradually, as the children grew, and we realized how very quickly the years passed, we videotaped less and less. One Christmas morning, Steve told me he would rather not tape the children as they ran into the family room, saw their piles of gifts from Santa, and jumped with delight. He wanted to see it as it unfolded, not from behind the lens of a video camera. We both realized that although videotaped memories are lovely to have, being present in the moment is much more special and important to us.

You see, when a person experiences something from behind a camera or from behind a phone, he or she misses the beauty and magic of actually experiencing the moment and becomes a spectator instead, merely observing, removed by the presence of a piece of technology. One cannot help but be distracted and less able to participate in the moment. Time passes quickly, and children grow before your eyes. The temptation to record and document every single moment is real, especially in this age of Instagram, Facebook, and other numerous social media outlets that continuously reward users for sharing pictures and videos of everyday lives.

If I could give advice to young mothers, I would encourage them to live in those happy, precious moments of childhood with their children. The moments that make our lives are the ones that are spontaneous and unedited. The best moments are the ones that happen without a camera in our child's face, creating a barrier between us. Enjoy the random giggles, the messy faces, the cozy snuggles. These moments are made just for you and your children. You can tuck them in your heart, and know they are safe there forever.

Please don't feel that because everyone else seems to be filming and posting and liking and sharing, you have to as well. You can choose to put the phone down and devote your time to being with your children. It's ok! I promise! In fact it's better than ok. The moments you share with your child are unique gifts. Once they're gone, you cannot get them back. Be there. Be with your children. Enjoy the moments. You will never regret it.

We have several little cassettes, all dated and numbered, in a box on the shelf in our storage area. Every now and again, we pull them out, put them in a converter, and play them in our old VCR. I know soon we'll have to convert them to DVD or Blu-ray or whatever comes next, but for now, we keep them as they are. Having those little moments documented is nice. But it's even sweeter to have the memories in our hearts.

Planning A Wedding

February 20, 2019

Years ago, when I was in college, my favorite professor and nun stated that to write well, one should write about what one knows. Right now, I know about planning a wedding. And I must say, contrary to popular belief, I found it to be fun and undaunting. Here, while they are fresh in my memory, are a few thoughts I have about planning a wedding.

Enjoy. Planning a wedding is as challenging and stressful as you make it. Our family decided early on that we would enjoy every part of this most special time in our daughter's life. We chose to work together and keep things as simple as we could. We thought about how important each aspect of the wedding was to Madison and Nicolas, and made decisions accordingly. For example, while flowers are an integral part of wedding festivities, Madison and Nicolas planned on celebrating their wedding a few hours from home and knew that getting fresh flowers from our local florist would be a difficult task. We didn't want to order from a florist we didn't know, and picking them up the day before, transporting them, and keeping them fresh was too much. Instead, Madison found an Etsy shop and worked with the owner to design the most lovely silk flowers that will last forever.

Recognize your strengths. And your weaknesses. In other words, do what you do, and let others do what they do. If designing and decorating is your thing, find an empty venue and go for it. If it isn't, find a place that will do it for you. And then let them do their job. We chose a venue that provided a lovely sit-down dinner. This sentence should read: The hotel manager was pleasantly surprised when he asked Madison to tell him where she wanted things placed on the table, and she responded that he could do it however he thought it should be. That is what he does. So, we let him do it. And it was amazing.

Resist the urge to fall into the Pinterest trap. Pinterest is great. And it is awful. Great because it offers so many ideas. Awful because it can create unrealistic expectations and unnecessary pressure. I encouraged Madison to let go of all those Pinterest pictures and think instead about what she and Nicolas wanted their day to look like. After all, no one on Pinterest shares their same ideas, interests, memories, moments, and thoughts. I encouraged them to forget all those pictures and expectations and enjoy the day they created.

Relax. Really. Remember that your guests are there because you invited them. You invited them because they are special to you and your child. They're not there to critique your choice of linens or count the different types of cookies you offer. These are the people you chose to celebrate the most special day in your child's life. Forget the stress and enjoy. I was so happy at Madison's wedding. Really happy. I was delighted to celebrate my girl and her new husband. I was also happy to honor and entertain the people we chose to share the day with us.

Unplug. Remember to enjoy all your planning. The day of the wedding, I gave Rhett my phone. I wanted to be in the moment. I soaked in every single smile, tear, hug, laugh, dance, visit, and kiss. I am so thankful I did. The day passes so quickly. I didn't want to miss a moment.

I know there are many more thoughts on planning a wedding. You can find them in any wedding book, binder, and of course on Pinterest. These are just a few of the things I am thinking of as I settle back into life after the wedding. I hope someday these little thoughts help you enjoy one of the most wonderful times of your life.

The End...For Now

While I have many more thoughts on motherhood, home, and family, I must end this somewhere! I hope these little passages brought some comfort, perspective, and joy to your day. I also hope to follow this with a little book sharing our love of all things holiday, and how we celebrate each one. Until then, you can read more on my blog, *Afternoon Coffee and Evening Tea.* Enjoy each moment with your loved ones, and don't forget that cup of afternoon coffee.

Made in the USA
Columbia, SC
12 December 2019

84765962R00059